PROP 8 OVERTURN

Alfredo Duran a.k.a. Chad Duran

iUniverse, Inc.
Bloomington

PROP 8 OVERTURN

iUniverse books may be ordered through booksellers or by contacting:

iUniverse
1663 Liberty Drive
Bloomington, IN 47403
www.iuniverse.com
1-800-Authors (1-800-288-4677)

ISBN: 978-1-4620-0393-8 (pbk)
ISBN: 978-1-4620-0394-5 (ebk)

Printed in the United States of America

iUniverse rev. date: 3/21/11

CHAPTER I

PROP 8 OVERTURN

August 4, 2010 was a highly anticipated day for those on both sides of the Prop 8 debate. The year and a half-long trial in the District Court of San Francisco was finally over. Judge Vaughn Walker was to announce his verdict between 1:00 p.m. and 4:00 p.m. that Wednesday. I was trying to download CNN to my computer so I could watch as it happened.

While fiddling around on the website, my cell phone rang. It was Connor, calling to remind me to turn on CNN. We had plans to go to a rally after the decision was announced, no matter what the outcome.

Frustratingly, I spent what seemed like a half-hour trying to download Adobe Flash so I could meet the system requirements to view the broadcast. Just as I was closing in on a channel, my phone rang. I answered it, "Hello, hello."

Connor was elated, and gave me the good news. "The judge ruled that Prop 8 is Unconstitutional, and overturned it!"

"I love life again!" I exclaimed. "I knew the propaganda that the traditional marriage side was pushing through the media would be shown to be just that: false. I have to go tell my mom. I'll see you soon."

I pushed the END button on my phone. I could feel the tears of joy running down my face as I ran into the living room.

"Prop 8 has been overturned," I declared.

"So now GLBT can get married again," replied my mom, Verna.

"Not quite yet, but it gives a positive outlook for the future. It won't be long until we find out when we can begin to marry again."

As I was hugging my mom, Connor pulled up. I ran out the door, ecstatic. The rally we were going to had turned into a celebration!

CHAPTER 2

THE NIGHT BEFORE THE NOVEMBER 4, 2008 ELECTION

Twenty-one months ago, Prop 8 was on the ballot. A campaign spearheaded by churches and traditional marriage supporters lobbied, and got a proposition on the ballot to ban same-sex marriage. I knew I had to do everything I could to stop this atrocity.

Three weeks prior to the election, I stepped my advocacy up to a higher level. I knew I had to be more outspoken; I made it a point to talk and discuss with nearly every person I came across. I campaigned at work, informing and educating my customers: it's not up to the Church to tell the State what it can and cannot do. I further explained that all the GLBT community wants is the right to enjoy the same privileges straight couples do. We want our marriage to be recognized and legally binding so we can be on each other's health insurance policy, or if something happened to one of us, the other had rights to carry out our final wishes. It's that simple.

Many of my customers were receptive and supportive. One such customer was a man who has been married for fifty years, who told me that, "What you do in your own house is your own business."

I replied, "Thank you, sir. I wish those damned Mormons shared your beliefs and were as open-minded as you."

While the old man was walking away, I was grinning from ear to ear. It was great that a man who was in a traditional marriage for so long was against Prop 8 and was supporting the right for others to have a non-traditional marriage.

This was November 3, 2008, the night before the election. I just knew that we were going to win. As a gay American, I was excited to get to go to the polls the next morning and have my voice be heard.

While lying in bed, a text beeped. It was from Ciara. "Chad, tomorrow at this time the GLBT will be able to get married."

I texted back. "Yes and all of us GLBT will be happy because we will defeat the traditional marriages." I pushed send on the message and the screen disappeared.

Just as I was dozing off, another text beeped. This one was from Cory. "Tomorrow GLBT will victorize."

I texted back. "Yes and tomorrow our GLBT community will prove to the churches and traditional marriages that we will get our civil and equal rights." I pushed send on the message and the screen disappeared. I laid back in my bed, anxious to fall asleep so I could go to the polls and cast my vote.

CHAPTER 3

ELECTION DAY

I woke around 6:00 a.m., an hour before the polls would be open, to the smell of fresh-brewed coffee coming from the kitchen. As I headed toward the kitchen with my "Hawaii" coffee mug, I passed my mom in the hallway.

"Don't forget to vote today, mom," I told her.

"I will go later; I'm voting for Obama and no on Prop 8," my mom replied.

"That is correct, mom. But the most important thing is no on Prop 8," I said.

I continued on into the kitchen and poured myself a cup of coffee. I went to the fridge, grabbed the milk, added it to my cup and stirred it in. I picked up my mug, took a sip, and walked back to my room. I took another drink. I grabbed my toothbrush and toothpaste and headed down the hall to the bathroom.

I turned on the water; it was scalding hot and burned my hand. I yelled, "The water is fucking hot! Who left the water on?" I got the water to the perfect temperature and washed my face. Next, I brushed my upper teeth and my lower teeth, and rinsed four or five times. I turned the water off and went back to my bedroom.

I put on my Levi's and white Hanes t-shirt. I put on tennis shoes since I had about a half-mile to walk. I sat down on my bed and checked my cell phone. I was surprised to see that I didn't have any new text messages. While I finished up my coffee, I was contemplating the impact my vote was going to have; at 10:00 p.m. tonight the GLBT will be able to marry their partners! After I finished my coffee, I checked my face in the mirror (to make sure there was no coffee on my mouth.) I combed my hair and headed into the living room.

"I'm walking up to the church to vote," I told my mom.

"Have a nice time voting. I'll see you home later," she replied.

I ran out the door. As soon as I stepped onto the porch, I realized that I didn't have my cell phone. I turned around and ran back into the house.

"Chad, slow down before you knock your step-dad down," warned my mom.

"I'm sorry mom, but I forgot my damned cell phone," I replied. I went into my room, and when I picked up my phone I saw that I had two text messages.

The first message was from Ciara. "I'm on my way to vote and I proposed to Cathy last night. Our marriages for the GLBT is one day away."

I texted back. "Heck yeah and now we will be just like our mothers and fathers, Amen."

The second message was from Cam. "I'm going to marry Arie on Saturday."

I texted back. "Who will be the bridesmaid?" I pushed send on the message and the screen disappeared.

I ran out the door, smiling with the knowledge that the GLBT will defeat the traditional marriages.

CHAPTER 4

AT THE POLLS

My polling precinct (location) is about a half-mile from my house on the south side of Eureka. I knew it was roughly a half-hour walk, round-trip. As I turned the corner onto Harris Street and felt the cold, brisk air on my face, I decided to light up a cigarette. I lit up the Marlboro, inhaling deeply. I released the smoke and thought a cigarette never tasted so good. Walking up Harris Street and smoking, I noticed very little traffic (on what is one of the busiest streets in Eureka.)

I walked past my brother Van's apartment, three blocks into my walk. The apartments looked pretty quiet. I did not see his, nor his girlfriend's car in the parking lot.

I continued my walk up the near-silent street. As I approached the church, I noticed a lot of cars in the parking lot. A woman got out of her car wearing a one-piece jump suit with black heels. I watched her scurry into the church and thought, *I hope I do not have to stand in line with these uptight Republicans who will be voting yes on Prop 8*. I followed the walkway up to the entrance and opened the door.

Right in front of me was a man on his way out; he was wearing a shirt with a "No on 8" slogan on the front. I thought to myself, *It must be a good omen, I'm glad it wasn't a Republican.* The man waved at me as we passed.

I walked up to the table where the Precinct Board was sitting. A woman in a red, white and blue t-shirt asked me, "May I have your first and last name?"

"Chad Duran," I replied.

"Here you go, Chad: your ballot, privacy sleeve, and pen. Now you may walk over to one of the booths," the Board Member instructed.

I had a huge smile on my face as I walked over to the booth because I knew that when this day was over, all of the GLBT community will have the right to marry. I stepped into the booth. There was a table with partitions separating me from the voters in the booths to either side of me. I set the ballot on the table, on top of the privacy sleeve. I grasped the pen in my right hand and got down to business.

I filled in the circle for the President and moved on to the local candidates. Next came the Propositions. I dutifully filled in the circles, with a special emphasis on Prop 8. I finished by voting on the measures. I slipped my ballot into the privacy sleeve, returned my pen to the table and headed over to the ballot box.

The man standing at the ballot box said, "Good morning. Just slide your ballot into the machine."

"Here it goes," I said. The ballot slid easily into the machine; I saw the counter on the screen increase by one. The man handed me my "I VOTED" sticker.

I ran out of the church, positive that Prop 8 would be defeated!

CHAPTER 5

VOTING RESULTS

The return walk from my polling location definitely felt quicker; I was walking on air. It seemed I had barely finished my cigarette and I was already home. I ran into the house and saw my mom getting ready to go vote. My mom put on her red sweater and headed out the door.

I had around a half-hour before I had to leave for work. I changed my shirt, put my "I VOTED" sticker on it, and decided to do my hair. Just as I squirted the gel into my hand, a text beeped on my phone.

It was from Mya. "After today I will go and marry my partner." Mya is a lesbian friend of mine who is half-white and half-African-American.

As I texted back, I was smiling real big. "We will win and win big. Oh yeah marriage is finally here for the GLBT." I pushed send on the message and the screen disappeared.

I finished getting ready and began the five-minute walk to work at the Rinky Dink mall. As I passed the grocery store, I noticed a lot of people wearing "I VOTED" stickers.

I continued walking and saw the female bum with the cat, sitting on the garbage can. As I neared her, she yelled, "You got any spare change?"

I replied, "Damn you! Stop harassing me for my hard-earned money. Go get a job."

I rounded the corner and saw my boss and a couple of guys from the freight crew smoking outside. As I approached, the guy in his fifties with glasses and curly brown hair pointed at his "I VOTED" sticker. He said, "Look, Chad. I went to vote."

"Cool, Donny. So did I. Did you vote no on Prop 8?"

"Chad, of course I voted no on Prop 8," Donny replied.

I walked into the store, clocked in, and got to work. While ringing up customers, my phone continuously beeped with new text messages.

One of my customers, Sheryl, is an old hippy woman. While I was ringing her up, she said to me, "Don't you worry, Chad. No on Prop 8 will win."

"You bet they will win, Sheryl. Then the GLBT community can marry," I replied.

"All I needed was this laundry soap."

"No problem. That will be one-oh-nine."

"Thank you, Chad. Have a good day."

"You too, Sheryl."

A few minutes later, my boss let me know it was time for my break. I put the "Closed Register" sign up, grabbed my phone and ran outside. I only had ten minutes to smoke and check my messages.

The first message was from Carl. "It is not looking good right now we should be way more ahead than what the numbers are showing."

The third message was from Dean. "Its not looking good." I flicked my cigarette and yelled loudly.

I walked slowly back inside to finish the last two hours of my shift. Those were the worst two hours I have ever had at work. No one was texting me, so I knew it had to be a bad sign. Work was extremely busy, and it seemed that every other customer was one of those church mothers, wearing those god-awful ugly skirts that go down past their knees, with their hair in a bun. Every time I rang one of them up I couldn't help wondering, *Where is your husband now? Probably with some other woman.*

I wanted eight p.m. to be here, and be here now. I looked at the clock on the wall; it read seven forty-five. That is when my manager walked up to me and told me I could go home.

I swear I smoked like six cigarettes on the five-minute walk home. As soon as I walked in, I turned the television on to the news. They reported that it was looking like Obama was a sweep for the Presidency. That made me happy, as the polls in the East were already closed. The forecast for Prop 8 infuriated me; Prop 8 was winning, forty-seven to forty-one. I just wanted to die.

Chapter 6

THE DAY AFTER VOTING
NO ON PROP 8

I woke up feeling extremely tired. I worried all night long, wondering what the morning news was going to report. I felt disoriented from lack of sleep and angry because of what I heard on the news last night. I sat up in my bed and tried to stretch and bend; stretching wasn't going to wake me up properly. I just ended up feeling like crap. I walked from my bedroom to the living room, where my mom was reading the local newspaper.

"Mom, I want to see the results for Prop 8," I told her.

"There on the couch are the results. All I know is that Obama is our new President," my mom stated.

"Mom, thank you so much," I told her as I kissed her on the cheek and grabbed the paper from the couch. I brought the paper into my room and jumped on my bed.

In big black letters, the front page of the paper proclaimed that Barack Obama was our new President. I turned the page to find out the results for Prop 8. I hoped that the unofficial results from last night were just a bad dream, and that we had won. As I read the official results, my pissed-off mood escalated to a murderous rampage: Prop 8 yes – fifty-two percent, Prop 8 no – forty-seven percent.

I ripped the newspaper in half as tears poured from my eyes. I threw myself on my bed, in the prone position, hitting my pillow and screaming.

A few minutes later, my phone beeped with a text from Connor. "They beat us, the Yes on Prop 8. Text me back please, Chad."

I texted back. "How did this happen? I think the propaganda commercial with the two parents and the little girl saying that gays will teach us about gay sex in school was one of the main false advertisements that helped the Yes on Prop 8 win." I pushed send on the message and the screen disappeared.

I lay on my bed, a pissed-off gay American living in California. The yes on Prop 8 just took away my rights as an American; I felt like a second-class citizen.

CHAPTER 7

MARRIAGE EQUALITY HOLDS A RALLY AT THE COURTHOUSE

The next day, I heard that there was going to be a rally at the courthouse. I also heard it had been organized by Stan, one of the top guys at the Humboldt County Marriage Equality Chapter. There was no way I would miss going to that rally. I wanted to let everyone know that I felt that my rights as an American had been taken away from me. I knew there would be signs at the rally that said, "MARRIAGE EQUALITY" and I wanted to hold one of those signs up so high! I wanted to show the world that this rally was just the beginning; I was just one of the many GLBT Americans in California who would win their rights back by protesting, holding rallies, and marching. I knew the truth would come out in the future, that the voters had been filled with the propaganda on television and didn't understand what they were truly voting for.

The morning of the rally I woke up, feeling like terrorists had just dropped an atomic bomb on the GLBT community.

I texted Connor. "Hey can you pick me up at 10 so we can go to the gay coffee house and get Lavender lattes." I pushed send on the message and the screen disappeared.

I quickly got in the shower, making sure that the water was hot. As I soaped my face and then my chest, I lifted my head up as the tears started to roll down my face. I still hadn't gotten over the shock of the outcome of the vote. Standing under the hot water with those thoughts in my head was nearly too much to bear. I slid down until I was sitting in the tub, with the water from the showerhead pouring over my face and body.

I cried and screamed, "This can't be right!" I sat in the tub until I was finally done with my crying fit. I stood up and turned off the water. I then grabbed my towel and wrapped it around my waist, walking to my bedroom, dripping wet.

As I was wiping my wet body off, my phone beeped with a text from Connor. "Dude I feel stripped of my American rights. I will see you at 10 with a sad smile."

I put on my army shorts, a green American Eagle t-shirt, and tennis shoes. I combed my long black hair, then laid prone on my bed with my face in the pillow. I was really hating everything at that moment. I was forty-seven years old and California chose yes on Prop 8. I thought that California was the most liberal state; now California is the eight equals hate state. Fuck everyone and fuck everything was how I was feeling.

Chapter 8

DRIVING TO THE COURTHOUSE

Connor and I arrived at The Cup, the only openly gay coffeehouse in Eureka, and each ordered a large Lavender Latte. Connor was wearing a *Fuck You* attitude like it was a neon sign. Nearly everything that came out of his mouth was, "Damn breeders," and, "Fuck California."

Finally I told him, "Connor, in ten minutes you and I will be at the courthouse with hundreds of other GLBT who are also angry."

"Chad, here is the key. Open your fucking door," he responded.

I opened my door. I could tell how angry my best friend was. He and his partner Tad were planning to get married when Tad got out of boot camp. The passing of Prop 8, which stripped and raped us of our rights, had had a huge effect on my best friend. I unlocked the driver's side door and Connor collapsed into his seat, bawling hysterically. I grabbed him and gave him a huge hug. I then pulled away a bit and took his chin in my hand and stared directly into his green eyes.

"Connor," I told him, "I'm here for you. I know that all you want is the right to marry Tad. I know how much marrying Tad would mean to you. I understand your anger and that you feel that California is a shitty conservative state. We were let down by the voters; I am angry too. I want to be able to get married when I find the right guy, just like you found Tad.

"Please look at me, Connor."

Connor looked over at me. I said, "Let's go to the courthouse and be with hundreds of others who feel the same way we do."

"I'm sorry about falling apart. You are right, let's go to the rally at the courthouse so we can show our pride and retaliate," he agreed.

His eyes were glassy and angry red; it really made his green eyes stand out. I told him, "In the long run, it will come out that the Yes on 8 campaign cheated and used scare tactics to win. We will find the truth in the future."

A few minutes later, we were driving up Fifth Street toward the courthouse. When we were a block away, we saw hundreds of protesters out in front of the courthouse. Connor and I looked at each other, and with huge smiles on our faces, said, "Marriage equality for all."

CHAPTER 9

AT THE COURTHOUSE

We parked about a block away, near the Carter House Inn. I pulled down the visor mirror to make sure there was no whipped cream hanging around from my latte. I passed inspection and pushed the visor back up.

"Dude, you ready to walk with hundreds of other GLBT?" Connor asked.

"Oh, yeah. Let's get out of this car and join them," I answered.

"Chad, make sure you grab the megaphone, and don't forget the cigarettes," Connor said as he got out of the car. He slammed the door hard; it was deafening.

As I got out of the car, I saw three lesbians and two gay men a quarter of a block away. They were walking with signs that said, "8 = HATE". Connor and I jogged to catch up with them. This was exactly what we needed; to be with hundreds of others like us who needed to do something, to be heard.

Fifth Street was packed, in front of the courthouse. I saw ten different signs. A few of the slogans were: "Marriage Equality", "Eight Equals Hate", and "We Want The Right To Marry Now". I reached out and grabbed his hand as we got closer. We were both smiling; I could see that he was feeling a lot better. I knew that protesting would make him feel like he was effecting change; the first steps to overturning Prop 8.

The noise was nearly overwhelming; it was so loud I'm sure they could hear us all the way to San Francisco! People were moving their signs up and down, walking in front of traffic and yelling. I tapped Connor on the shoulder.

"Dude, let's go get a 'Marriage Equality' sign and march around the block. We can raise our signs and be proud gay boys," I said.

"Yes, let's do this," he replied.

And for an hour, we did.

CHAPTER 10

AT THE GAY BAR

After the march, those of us who were over twenty-one planned to go to Aunty Mo's, the only gay bar in town. We were really looking forward to a good, stiff whiskey. We decided to walk the four blocks from the courthouse to the bar, as we were likely to have more than three drinks apiece. As we walked, we talked about the march and mused on what the next step would be, on the road to getting Prop 8 overturned. Connor's attitude was like day from night; he no longer felt helpless and alone. Instead of just responding to my questions, he was actually engaged in the conversation. He elucidated his feelings on the issues surrounding the passing of Prop 8.

We were approaching the Indian restaurant. We decided to sit on the bench out front, and have a smoke. Connor dropped his backpack on the ground and we sat down on the bench. I got two Marlboros out of my pack and handed one to Connor.

"Do you have a light?" Connor asked. I lit a match for him and he lit his cigarette; the flame was big enough for me to light mine with the same match, as well.

"I think that this march has given a positive outlook for the GLBT community in Eureka. It certainly has given me hope. It also made me realize that it's not just about marriage equality, it's more than that. It's about our rights as American citizens," said Connor.

"You're right, it's about separating the church from the state. It's about the people. Right now we're feeling like second-class citizens, like we're not free. The only way the GLBT can overcome this atrocity, to overturn Prop 8, is by continuing to advocate for marriage equality. Marriage is the same, whether straight or gay. We need to march, we need to be heard," I told him.

A couple of queers, Matt and Greg stopped at the bench while we were deep in conversation.

"Hi Chad, Connor," they said.

"Hey, Matt."

"Hey, Greg."

"It was good to see you two marching at the courthouse," Matt said.

"Thanks, you too. We'll see you inside in a few minutes," I said.

Connor and I finished our cigarettes and walked to the bar.

Aunty Mo's is a two-story bar. When you enter there is the podium with the cash register and I.D. check. Then, you can either go to the right and head toward the dance floor, or to the left and head toward the bar. Connor and I went to the left. As we stepped to the bar, a microphone screeched with feedback.

CHAPTER 11

THE SPEECH ON THE STAGE AT THE BAR

Connor and I ordered whiskey and Cokes. When we got them, we decided to do a toast.

"Marriage equality for all!" After we clinked glasses, we both took a sip. Man, did that bartender make some stiff drinks!

"I think this is a glass of whiskey with a shot of Coke," I sputtered.

"At least we're getting our money's worth," he replied.

As Connor and I were making our way toward the dance floor, we passed a group of lesbians who were huddled together at the bar. They appeared to be plotting to overthrow an evil dictator, or planning battle strategy for a war. At the end of the bar, we passed a group of guys wearing "Marriage Equality" t-shirts. They all waved and smiled at us as we walked by.

The dance floor was packed and there was a guy on stage, near the microphone. He was wearing a "Marriage

Equality" t-shirt and wire-rimmed glasses. He kept pressing his lips together. Connor pointed out a large couch to the left of the stage where we could sit. Sitting on one end of the couch was a guy with a shaved head with an "8 = HATE" t-shirt and a backpack on. His boyfriend was sitting on his lap, and was wearing the same shirt.

"Hey, do you guys mind if we occupy the rest of the couch space?" Connor asked them.

"That will be fine," the one with the backpack said. "The more, the merrier."

Just as we sat down, a different guy wearing a "Marriage Equality" t-shirt and Levi's began speaking into the microphone (he had a straw hat.)

"My name is Frank and I'm in charge of the Humboldt County Marriage Equality Chapter. I would like to thank all of my GLBT brothers and sisters who came out and supported the march. I want all of you GLBT to recognize that this is just the beginning and we will all continue to fight for equality."

I looked around and everybody was paying attention, really listening. Frank continued his speech, about how it was a close race, and how we need to separate church and state. He concluded his speech, informing everyone where the Marriage Equality Chapter was located, and that if anyone was interested in joining, he would be near the pool tables with a sign-up sheet.

CHAPTER 12

CONNOR AND CHAD
LEAVE FOR S.F.

Within the six months after Proposition 8 passed, many different organizations for equal rights had been formed. Chad Griffin founded AFER (American Foundation for Equal Rights), which helps support GLBT in their fight for the right to marry. Griffin was going to be in San Francisco representing both a gay couple and a lesbian couple who felt their civil rights had been violated and felt they were being classified as second-class citizens. They went to the courts to have a trial and get Prop 8 overturned. Connor called to tell me about it.

"Hey Chad, do you want to go to San Francisco with me for the weekend? We can go shopping and see if there is going to be a protest outside of the courthouse for the couples that are trying to overturn Prop 8."

"I would love to. We are from middle-class families, but feel like second-class citizens. We should go support them. There's no stopping us now!" I replied.

Connor picked me up at six o'clock the next morning. I grabbed my suitcase, and gave my mom a hug.

"Mom, Connor and I are leaving now to go to San Francisco," I reminded her. "We're going to go protest, to support the overturn of Prop 8. I will be back on Sunday."

"Now you be careful Chad and have a good protest," she replied.

I heaved my suitcase into the backseat and got in the front. Connor was yawning; his hair was all gelled and he was wearing a white tank top, khaki shorts and flip-flops.

"All right, let's go!" Connor exclaimed. He started the engine, put the car in gear, and we were on our way to join thousands of GLBT and fight for our rights.

CHAPTER 13

CONNOR AND CHAD IN S.F.

The road trip took around six hours. We rented a hotel room at Granada Suites, on Market and Powell. As soon as we got in the room, we collapsed on our beds for around an hour. I was the first to wake up. It was 3:00 p.m. I grabbed my room key and headed to the Starbucks, two blocks away.

Out front was a man selling *The San Francisco Chronicle*. Right there on the front page was a headline stating that the Plaintiffs were in San Francisco for the hearing to fight for the overturn of Prop 8. I bought a paper for a dollar fifty. I rolled it up, put it under my arm and walked into Starbucks.

The line was long, but it moved fast. Most of the customers were wearing suits and ties, very corporate. When I got up to the counter, I ordered a white mocha for myself, and a caramel latte for Connor.

While I was waiting for my order to come up, I looked at the paper. I overheard two gay guys talking about the march in front of the courthouse. I looked over at them;

one with dark hair, dark eyes and a medium build, the other with blond hair, blue eyes and slender. The dark-haired guy told the blond guy to make sure that he got off work early so they could go to the march.

When the barista called my name, I jumped up grabbed my coffees and headed back to the hotel. On the walk back, I saw lots of people wearing "Marriage Equality" t-shirts. I felt so happy to be in a big city, where the GLBT community is larger than the population of my hometown.

When I walked into the lobby of the hotel, I saw Connor at the front desk. I walked up to him and handed him his coffee drink. He was getting directions to the courthouse for tomorrow. The hotel clerk drew him a map and everything!

CHAPTER 14

A SURPRISE INVITE FOR CONNOR FROM AFER

Early the next morning, the phone rang. I picked it up.

"Hello."

"Hello, this is the front desk. May I speak to a Connor Williams?"

"Connor is sleeping, it is barely eight a.m. Why are you calling for Connor?" I asked.

"There is an invitation to an after-party for the people who are attending the rally at the courthouse. It is at the front desk waiting for Connor Williams."

"When he wakes up, I will give him the message, ma'am," and hung up the phone.

I went into the bathroom to wash my face, hoping it would wake me up. I splashed water on my face, then looked in the mirror. Boy, did I look tired! I splashed more water on my face. I heard Connor moving around.

"Good morning, fag. You ready for the march today?" he asked.

"Yeah, you faggot. Do you think there will be a lot of people?" I asked.

""I'm sure there will be. All of the Bay Area and peninsula will be there to cheer for the couples who are trying to overturn Prop 8."

"Oh Connor, the front desk called this morning. They said they have an invitation with your name on it; it's for an event after the rally."

"Who in the hell sent me an event invitation?"

"How would I know? Wait a minute, haven't you been online, chatting with people about going to the rally here in San Francisco?"

"You're right. I joined AFER; everyone who signed up gets to attend the rally that's going to be held after the march."

"So, do you want to shower first?"

"Yes, but I want to pick out some cute clothes first." He decided on shorts, a tank top, and flip-flops.

While I was waiting for my turn in the shower, I was thinking about the rally. It had been six months since Prop 8 passed and again, I would be protesting in front of a courthouse. Only this time, it would be a way larger courthouse, in a way larger city, with a way larger crowd. Also, this was more like supporting, than it was protesting. This rally was going to be a pivotal event in my life and I knew it would be an historical event, marking the path to the overturn of Prop 8. I would be attending not just for myself, but also for all my friends who couldn't be there.

CHAPTER 15

AT THE COURTHOUSE IN S.F.

The crowd at the courthouse was enormous. This was just the first meeting with the Plaintiffs (from Los Angeles and Berkley) to overturn Prop 8. The crowd was chanting, "Marriage Equality Now!" The noise was so loud that an old bag lady yelled, "Shut the fuck up!" as she walked by, pushing her cart.

As Connor and I crossed the street, I held onto his pocket so we didn't get separated in the mob. We wanted to find signs, so I asked where to get one from a guy who was holding an "8 Equals Hate" sign. He told us to walk up the steps and go to the right.

We walked quickly up the stairs. From the top all I could really make out were the signs moving up and down, since the crowd was packed so tightly. Unfortunately, there were no more signs left. Just then, we heard a guy announce on a megaphone, "Well, it looks like the judge ruled in favor of the Plaintiffs. There will be more details in the months to follow."

It was only 3:00 p.m. and we had only been there for half an hour. The meeting was already over, but the outcome was in our favor! It was another step with a positive outcome for the GLBT. In my heart, I still felt that the churches had gotten Prop 8 passed illegally. I must have been somewhere else in my head, because all of a sudden I realized that Connor was shaking me really hard.

I then heard him say, "Chad, did you hear that? The judges ruled in favor of the Plaintiffs?"

"Yeah, yeah!" I replied.

"Chad, wake up! This means that there is hope for me to marry my husband when he gets out of the military!"

"I'm so happy for you! I know this means everything to you, to marry your husband."

Tears of joy were running down his face. I grabbed him and looked him in the eyes, "There is a god," I said. "That god is Harvey Milk and he is watching over this crowd of thousands, filled with joy."

"You are so right. Let's go celebrate!"

The crowd slowly filtered out, leaving in all directions. There was an aura of hope that I couldn't help but feel. Connor and I were holding hands as we left the courthouse to find our way to the celebration.

CHAPTER 16

THE CELEBRATION

The celebration was not at all what we had expected; I had figured on drinks and dancing. It was at a house in Noe Valley, over the hill from the Castro district. It was a three-story house, and each story had the same DVD playing. The DVD was about gay men born in the United States and their status quo.

"Are you feeling as awkward as I am at this celebration?" Connor asked me.

"Yes. I thought everyone would be drinking and dancing," I replied.

We made our way back down to the second floor, which was the living room. It felt cozy and warm, and there were big couches. We sat on the same couch as these two preppy-looking queers, one in a Lacoste shirt and one in a Polo shirt. Across from us was a group of guys: some had suits on, others wore Levi's, some had moustaches, others were clean cut.

Connor scooted over closer to me and asked, "Do you want to dash for the door, or what?"

"If you want to leave, that's fine with me," I replied.

Just as we were about to stand up and head for the door, a man with salt-and-pepper hair walked into the room. He turned the DVD off, and began to speak very loudly in a totally gay voice.

"My name is Carl and I'm one of the guys who are responsible for this celebration at this beautiful Noe Valley home. I want to thank all of the GLBT for coming to our celebration. Our purpose is to talk with everyone here, and discuss how our civil rights were violated by the traditional marriage proponents in the November 2008 election. I have a form that will help us find out how many here in this room are born American Citizens. If there are no questions, I will pass these forms around the room."

Carl passed the forms to the left. When I got mine, I filled it out. The first question was, "What is your name?" *Chad Duran*. The second question was, "Are you a citizen or not a citizen?" *Citizen*. The third question was, "What state do you live in?" *California*. Connor and I finished filling out our forms at the same time and brought them up to Carl. We then walked out onto the balcony, to discuss the form.

"This form is going to help show how many gay Americans feel that justice has been denied to them in California," Connor said.

We both agreed that all of the questions were about being an American Citizen. We smoked our cigarettes and quietly left the celebration, still feeling like second-class citizens because of our loss to traditional marriages.

CHAPTER 17

CONNOR AND CHAD TALKING WITH A TRADITIONAL MARRIAGE COUPLE IN EUREKA

As the months passed by, Connor and I worked hard to keep our selves occupied. We tried not to think about Prop 8 very much. I was working five days a week, trying to hold on to my sanity.

It was especially hard when a customer made a joke about how he was so happy to be divorced. He boasted that he had had three wives, and divorced all three of them. Every time I heard a straight man talk about how many different wives they had had, it made me so angry that the GLBT couldn't even get married.

It had been a week since I had last seen Connor, so we made plans to meet up for coffee at Border's. I could hardly wait to see what was new with my best friend. I looked at my watch, and it was three fifty-eight. Only two minutes until my shift was over.

At four o'clock my boss told me it was time to count my till.

"Sweet," I replied. "I'm ready to get out of here."

My till was a couple of cents short, but that was no big deal. I clocked out, and walked to Border's.

It took about ten minutes to walk there. It was a pretty dull walk; there weren't even any people yelling obscene words as they drove past me, while I walked down the hill. The streetlight at the bottom of the hill was green, so I hurried across the street. I walked across the parking lot of the Upbeat Mall, to Border's. I walked through the double doors. To the left, I heard a cashier ringing up a purchase. I continued on, heading to the rear of the store (where the coffee bar is.)

Connor was already there. He was chatting with a man in a suit and a woman in a pink dress. Connor waved to me. I walked over to the table and asked him if he wanted a caramel latte.

"I already have one, just go ahead and get your white mocha," he replied.

It took about five minutes, but I got my white mocha. I walked back over to Connor's table and sat down.

"Chad, this is Mr. And Mrs. Wright and we have been talking about Prop 8," he informed me.

"Cool. Nice to meet you both," I replied.

"The Wrights believe that a marriage between a man and a man or a woman and a woman is no different that between a man and a woman."

"That's awesome! Maybe at our next rally, they can speak about how they are for same sex marriages."

"The matter of the fact is that if two people love each other and want to share the same foundation of home, family, and religion, who has the right to stop them from marrying?" Mr. Wright said.

"Well, obviously that's how the GLBT feel, Mr. Wright, but as we all saw in the November 2008 elections, California didn't agree," I replied. "If all people in traditional marriages felt like you and were on our side, we would be allowed to marry and California would be a better state."

CHAPTER 18

MY NEIGHBOR MARY

I have lived in the same neighborhood for twenty years. The house across the street has had three or four different owners during that time. It's a pretty quiet neighborhood; most of the homeowners are in their sixties. I know most everyone in my neighborhood and they know me.

Today was extremely strange. The lady who lives across the street usually waters her lawn in the early morning and is usually doing some kind of handy work on her house; hammering nails, painting. I never really pay any attention to her because she is always in her own world. Sometimes in the morning I hear her yelling at her grandchildren to get out of the street or yelling at the dogs. It's funny, because I have heard the dogs barking, then like a minute after they stop, I will hear her loud voice yelling, "Shut up, Fido! Quit your barking!"

As I was walking home from work, I passed by her house and she yelled, "Hey! Are you my neighbor that lives across the street?"

"Yes, I'm Chad. I have lived in this house for twenty years," I replied.

"My name is Mary," she stated.

"Like the Mary who Jesus was married to," I replied, jokingly.

"Well, yeah. But you don't have to be that proper."

"Oh, Mary. I was just trying to be funny."

"So, I noticed that you had some signs in your yard that said, 'Separate the Church and State' and 'Marriage Equality' a while ago."

"That is correct. I went to a rally at the courthouse to protest Prop 8."

"Chad, can you tell me a little about Prop 8? I'm a preacher and I've been marrying people for ten years."

"Have you ever married same-sex couples?"

"Of course I have"

"That's great! Prop 8 was passed in the November 4, 2008 election. The traditional marriages stopped same-sex couples from getting married. Now many of us GLBT are trying to get our civil rights back."

"So, the people who believe in traditional marriages have been forcing their beliefs upon the state?"

"Pretty much. Ever since Prop 8 passed, our marriages became null and void."

"I hear my granddaughter screaming. I would like to continue this conversation some other time. Just stop by my house sometime and we'll have a cup of tea."

As I walked across the street to my house it really made sense, the Prop 8 issue. It wasn't just that we are GLBT and want the right to marry, it was also about justice and equality.

CHAPTER 19

AUGUST 3, 2010

Connor called and told me that the decision of whether or not Prop 8 would be overturned was to be announced the next day. What this meant was that if the judge were to overturn Prop 8, it would be because it was Unconstitutional. This was what we were all praying for.

Connor was going to pick me up in half an hour; I needed to get a move on. I washed my face with peach scrub, then I brushed my teeth. I smiled at my reflection in the mirror and said, "I pray that the judge overturns Prop 8."

My phone beeped with new text messages. The first message was from Corwin. "There will be a rally tomorrow in front of the courthouse at 5:30 for the Prop 8 overturn held by Lisa from PFLAG." I pushed end on the message and the screen disappeared.

That sounded cool. PFLAG is an organization for the *Parents, Families and Friends of Lesbians and Gays*. I figured I would text him back later.

The next text was from Aaron. "Don't forget the judge is ruling the Prop 8 overturn tomorrow." I pushed end on the message and the screen disappeared.

I dressed in Levi's and a green, long-sleeved American Eagle shirt. I slipped on my clogs and combed my hair. My phone rang; it was Connor.

"Dude, I'm outside."

"Sweet. I'll be right out," I replied.

I grabbed my bag and ran out the front door.

"Connor," I said, "Lisa from PFLAG is going to hold a rally at five-thirty at the courthouse."

"I have to work tomorrow," he replied.

"So do I, but let's call in sick. You in Connor?"

"I'm in. How about a drive to Trinidad?"

"Trinidad? What's there?"

"Shut up, Chad. We need a mellow drive; tomorrow is the big day for the judge to overturn Prop 8."

"If the overturn happens, everyone will know that we are American Citizens, due the same rights as everyone else. Everyone will be walking around, grinning from ear-to-ear."

CHAPTER 20

PROP 8 WAS OVERTURNED AND RULED UNCONSTITUTIONAL

On August 4, 2008, Prop 8 was overturned. The Chief Justice of the United States District Court in San Francisco deemed it Unconstitutional. The Plaintiffs from Los Angeles and Berkley won! The minute I received the phone call from Connor, the phone slipped out of my hands. I quickly picked it back up, while tears of joy streamed down my face.

"Get your ass over here, now," I told him.

"I'm on my way," he replied.

There is nothing in this world that I had ever wanted more, than for Prop 8 to be overturned. Our civil rights were won back, after a year and a half-long battle in court. The church and Yes on 8 campaign spent big money to manipulate California voters, and it was all for nothing! There was nothing they could do now that we got our ruling. It was a blessing to know that god does believe in justice and equality.

The Plaintiffs helped to make the GLBT community stronger. As American Citizens, all we want is the right to marry our partners; we want equality. We want the traditional marriages to understand that we work, pay taxes, raise children, and own homes the same as they do. The GLBT community will have the right, as partners to our home, car, and money when we die. Thank you, Judge Walker from San Francisco, for making the truthful decision, overturning Prop 8 because it was Unconstitutional. Thank you, Plaintiffs for sticking with it, through the long court battle.

I am a middle-aged gay man living in California. I am from a Catholic family, raised by a Hawaiian mother. I lost my Filipino father at a young age. I was born in Maui, and have lived in California since the age of four. I was taught that in California, there is equality for everyone. I have a degree from a California State University. I believe that if we do not protest, speak up for our gay rights, and vote, then we will never be heard.

My phone rang. It was Connor. "I'm outside your house."

"I'll be right out," I replied.

Connor was leaning against his car. I ran up to him and we hugged so hard. We were both crying.

"Now you can marry Tad!" I exclaimed.

"I can't wait to tell him, when he calls me later!"

"Today, justice and equality was our victory. It seems like our voices were heard, through the Plaintiffs. This is a giant leap forward for the GLBT community. August 18, 2010 is when we can marry again."